ZIONION

ZIONION

Why does the World obsess over Israel?

STEVE MALTZ

Saffron Planet
PO Box 2215
Ilford IG1 9TR
UK
T: +44 (0) 208 551 1719
E: contact@saffronplanet.net

ISBN 978-0-9931910-6-0

CONTENTS

Chapter 1:   Truth   7

Chapter 2:   What's with ... the British government?   9

Chapter 3:   What's with ... the Palestinians?   15

Chapter 4:   What's with ... the United Nations?   21

Chapter 5:   What's with ... the media?   27

Chapter 6:   What's with ... the activists?   31

Chapter 7:   What's with ... the academics?   37

Chapter 8:   What's with ... the boycotters?   43

Chapter 9:   What's with ... some Jews?   48

Chapter 10: Now it gets personal   52

Chapter 11: What's with ... jihadists?   54

Chapter 12: What's with ... the Christians?   58

Chapter 13: What's with ... neo-Nazis?   63

Chapter 14: What's with ... Conspiracy buffs?   67

Chapter 15: What's with ... ?   72

Chapter 16: Consequences   77

CHAPTER 1

Truth

There is a kind of inherited madness that affects many people. It clouds their thinking, stimulates their emotions and often provokes them into action. It's a madness because there is no logic in it, no single justification for it, yet it speaks with a sinister elegance, often with disastrous consequences. It is often denied because it can be clever at disguising itself, like a particularly nasty virus, yet it lurks in dark places, always ready to spring into action, when the conditions are right to do so.

It goes by the name of *anti-Semitism*, succinctly described as 'the longest hatred'. It has been around for over 4,000 years, ever since the Jewish people left the desert to live in communities, albeit as slaves to a rather horrid Pharaoh. It may have found its dominant expression in *religion* but it has learned to adapt and incredibly finds a home in virtually every aspect of human endeavour, as we shall see as this story develops.

The purpose of this little book is to expose the layers of hatred, as if peeling an onion, to shed light on the variety of aspects, scenarios and environments that this hatred has infiltrated. Each layer may be viewed as an oddity, or an unfortunate quirk, but, as the peeling gathers pace, the evidence of madness becomes undeniable as we witness perhaps the most insidious unspoken conspiracy in the history of mankind. Truth outstrips fiction as right-minded people collectively declare, 'you couldn't make this up!'

Indeed you couldn't, which is why most pertinent facts presented in this book are from the mouths, pens or actions of the protagonists, with commentary provided where necessary.

Let the story begin. We start by looking at the actions of the British government near the start of the 20th Century ...

CHAPTER 2

What's with …
the British government?

The relationship between the UK and the Jewish people has been a series of peaks and troughs, with the latter sadly pre-eminent. Nearly every peak, though welcome, had been inspired by selfish interests. In 1066, when England had become an outpost of France, the Jews were brought in not to rescue them from persecution, but as accountants and financiers to run the country. In 1656 Cromwell may have been partially motivated by religious zeal, but his acceptance of the Jewish exiles back into the country had everything to do with the expectation of a ready-made spying network against his continental enemies.

The only exception to this sorry situation was during the late 19th Century, when Britain opened its arms to help rescue the rejected and persecuted Jewish refugees from Russia and Eastern Europe, fleeing the pogroms. Their motivation mainly came from the *philo-Semitism* of prominent Christians such as Lord Shaftesbury, William Hechler and Charles Spurgeon as well as the fact that, in contrast with France and Germany, anti-Semitism was taking a breather. England, after all, now had a Jewish Prime Minister (albeit a baptised one!) in Benjamin Disraeli, as well as a smattering of Jewish knights, barons, Mayors and Lords. In fact, Queen Victoria was quite positively inclined towards her Jewish subjects.

When she died, things began to change. The Aliens Act

of 1905 was passed to limit Jewish immigration, the first sign that anti-Semitism was striving to gain a fresh foothold in the new Century. Then came the First World War, when fighting in the battle fields obscured the machinations that were taking place behind the scenes, in darkened rooms, desert tents and dusty palaces. With eyes looking forward to a post-war world, attention was firmly on the lands of the Middle East, currently held by the Turks. Trade routes had to be protected ... and then there was oil.

On May 26th 1908 the first major oilfield in the Middle East had been discovered in Persia by a British company. This was the Anglo-Persian Oil company, now known as *British Petroleum* (BP). And so this particular story begins, the subtext for much of the strife that has enveloped that region ever since. Britain had a foothold, but how would it continue to be a player in this global game? It was going to have to win battles ... and do deals.

It did a deal with the Arabs, in a series of letters from Sir Henry McMahon, British High Commissioner in Egypt, to the Sharif of Mecca, a powerful Arab leader in 1915. It promised Arab independence after the war was won, in return for help in the actual winning of the war. At the same time, British diplomat Mark Sykes was drawing up plans with the French and Russians to carve up the Middle East once the Turks were defeated. The third agreement regarding the same piece of land was made with the Jews, the *Balfour Declaration* in 1917.

Here we have some key political origins of the current conflict in the Middle East, the machinations of western politicians during the First World War, mainly from Britain. The cause of all this, as it always is with politicians, was *national self-interest*, for which every winner is at the expense of a loser (or losers). The winners were, at least for a few decades, these western politicians, as the flow of oil at a cheap price was ensured. But, as for the losers ...

After the war the land was carved up by the British and the French, *breaking the agreement with the Arabs*, forming the artificial states of Iraq and Syria. Then, three quarters of the land promised to the Jews was taken away from them, giving birth to another artificial state, Jordan (then called TransJordan), *thus breaking the agreement with the Jews.*

The good relationship developed between Britain and the Jews in Victorian times had been broken at the negotiators table and when push came to shove, political expediency dictated that the flow of oil was preferable to the dictates of natural justices, even when unsettling and sinister stories were coming out of Germany, now under a new regime!

Ever since the signing of the *Balfour Declaration* in 1917, the dealings of the British Government with the Jewish people had taken a downward trajectory. It is no secret that, for all the wars and skirmishes between Jews and Arabs since then, British actions have usually veered towards whoever served their best interests. Ever since Britain carved up the Middle East it has been cultivating relationships with the Arab ruling families, educating them at British colleges and Universities, such as Oxbridge and Sandhurst, leading to strong bonds with the upper classes and royal family. In the 1920s and leading up to the Second World War, Britain was given the mandate to rule the area of Palestine and its heavy-handed treatment of the Jews is well documented. Especially shameful was the Exodus incident in 1947, when a ship packed with Holocaust survivors was refused embarkation in Palestine and the survivors sent back to Europe, many ending up in Germany of all places.[1] This attitude is despite the fact that Britain had imposed a 75,000 limit on Jewish immigration just before the war, a quota that was never fulfilled, despite clear indications as to what had been happening in Nazi Germany.[2]

What we need to know now is the current situation, as this will provide clues as to what the future holds. Surely Middle Eastern dynamics have shifted, with power – for good or bad – resting in the nations and people themselves? The rise of militant Islam is also a major factor. Is the British Government still holding to the old colonial ties or have most of them now been broken as a result of the upheavals of the Arab Spring and what followed?

Getting straight to the point, what is the current policy of the British Government towards the State of Israel? Even if members of the Foreign Office have stopped parading through Westminster corridors in full Arab regalia, as some did in the 1930s, is it still fundamentally *arabist*?

We must look at evidence; voting patterns, public (and private) declarations, always remembering that actions speak louder than words. On the positive side, Prime Minister Theresa May revealed in December 2016 that Britain will become one of the first countries to adopt a definition of anti-Semitism that had been worded by the *International Holocaust Remembrance Alliance*. She said: *"It is unacceptable that there is anti-Semitism in this country. It is even worse that incidents are reportedly on the rise. As a government we are making a real difference and adopting this measure is a ground-breaking step. It means there will be one definition of anti-Semitism – in essence, language or behaviour that displays hatred towards Jews because they are Jews – and anyone guilty of that will be called out on it."*[3]

On the other hand, two years earlier, in October 2014, the House of Commons did vote overwhelmingly to recognise the Palestinian state, a non-binding act, but highly symbolic in the context of their understanding of the Israel/Palestine issue.[4]

The fact that only 12 MPs voted against the motion was a telling one. Equally telling was the fact that the UK voted against Israel in a UN resolution on Jerusalem that referred to Israel as the "occupying power" and that Israeli laws concerning Jerusalem were illegal and null and void.[5]

Just stop and think about this. Regardless of opinions of politicians in other nations, Jerusalem is Israel's chosen capital city, as it was 3,000 years ago, when London and every other major capital did not exist. Doesn't a nation have a right to declare its capital city, even if the city in question had changed hands in the past, depending on who ruled the land at the time?

What right does any other country have to decide on these matters?

What we learn from this is that the British government still continues to view the State of Israel through the lens of diplomacy and accepted consensus, even if this is not necessarily founded on objective truth, but rather influenced by the need to maintain good relations with nations that have the capacity to create serious bother or spoil the delicate equilibrium that maintains our World.

And what is the objective truth regarding Jerusalem? It is the eastern part of the city that is in dispute. Eastern Jerusalem was liberated (or conquered) by Israel in June 1967 in the *Six-Day War*. Before then it was held by Jordan, who controlled it as the spoils of the 1948-9 *War of Independence* and then annexed it in 1950 (an act condemned by all nations except Britain and Pakistan). Before then it was part of the British Mandate since 1923. Before that it was part of the Ottoman Empire. We can slip back through history and watch Jerusalem change hands again and again. The truth is that, regardless of the agenda-ridden proclamations of the United Nations and international community, East Jerusalem, *as with every area of the Earth*, belongs to the country that occupies it ... *Israel*. Now there's a loaded term. The reason why Israel 'occupies' it rather than 'inhabits' it is that, unlike any other conquering power, it chose *not* to drive out all those who were living there. And when the Old City of Jerusalem was liberated they chose to leave the mosques on the Temple mount intact, in contrast to the Jordanians who destroyed virtually every synagogue in Jerusalem when they were the occupying power.

These days we tend to peer at the World through a cloud of prejudice, political correctness and agenda, rather than insisting on a clear line of sight to the heart of the issue. It is fact we need to consider and not opinion. The fact is that the British Government, masters of diplomacy, choose the latter rather than the former, because that is the way the World runs. It would take a brave administration to buck this trend, but one never knows.

In the next chapter we look closer at the situation created by the British and others and, in particular, at the Palestinians themselves ...

NOTES
The web links from the notes at the end of each chapter can also be found at www.zionion.com

1   https://en.wikipedia.org/wiki/SS_Exodus
2   https://en.wikipedia.org/wiki/White_Paper_of_1939
3   https://www.gov.uk/government/news/government-leads-the-way-in-tackling-anti-semitism
4   https://www.theguardian.com/world/2014/oct/14/israel-condemns-british-mps-vote-palestinian-state
5   http://www.cufi.org.uk/news/uk-votes-against-israel-at-un/

CHAPTER 3

What's with ...
the Palestinians?

The dictionary description of a *narrative* is a "spoken or written account of connected events, a story". Until recently, the only time I have heard this term used outside of the world of fiction and drama is in regards to the history of the Israel/Palestine conflict in the 20th Century. There can only be one set of events that describes that history, yet there are *two conflicting narratives*, the Israeli one and the Palestinian one. Can they both be right? Aren't they just different interpretations of the same events? Well, there are not just different interpretations, but there's also disagreement on the actual events themselves!

Objectivity has given way to debate, where one's position is determined by where your sympathies lie. In 1986 a pivotal book on the subject was published. It was *From Time Immemorial*, by an American journalist, Joan Peters. The main point argued in the book was that most Palestinians were immigrants themselves and therefore have no claim to the disputed territory. There was immediate acceptance of the book from those who took the Israeli narrative, such as Saul Bellow, Barbara Tuchman and Elie Wiesel, but vitriolic rebuttal from others, particularly Norman Finkelstein, Noam Chomsky and Edward Said. The two positions are characterised by their view of the events of 1948. To the Israelis it was the triumph in the War of Independence, to the

Palestinians it was the *Nakba*, "the catastrophe of the creation of the State of Israel".

So, what do we make of this, when there can't even be agreement over the basic facts and where both sides regularly demonise the other? In the short space we have in this chapter we will not focus on opinions or even (contested) facts, but *the actions triggered by these facts and opinions*. It will then be up to you to consider these actions and arrive at your own conclusions regarding this critical situation in the Middle East.

Let us first examine the lives of both sets of populations in 1948 and compare the situation in general terms with the situation today. Firstly, the Arab inhabitants. To be historically accurate, they weren't called *Palestinians* at that time, this term referred to both Jews and Arab inhabitants. In fact the Jewish-owned *Jerusalem Post* newspaper was called the *Palestinian Post* until 1950. These Arabs were first identified as *Palestinians* in terms of a national movement in the 1960s, promoted mainly through Yasser Arafat and the *Palestinian Liberation Organisation* (PLO). In 1948 they were living mainly in villages, but also in urban areas. There had been close to a million living in the area of the current State of Israel, of which between 700,000 and 750,000 had left their homes by 1949, according to an Arab website.[1]

These became known as the Palestinian refugees. The official United Nations figure in 1950 was 711,000.[2] Of this total, between 30,000 and 50,000 were still alive in 2012, *over 60 years living as a refugee* in United Nations camps.[3] The total number of refugees had grown to around 1.5 million in 2012[4], *still living in refugee camps* in Gaza, the West Bank, Syria, Lebanon and, with by far the biggest numbers, in Jordan.[5]

Let's compare with the other people living in the land in 1948, the Jews. In the year before, there were 630,000 living there, including many who had survived the Nazi Holocaust in Europe.[6] Also, between this time and the early 1970s, around 850,000 Jews left Arab countries becoming the "forgotten refugees".[7] They left because, despite many having ancestral homes going back centuries in places like Iraq, Yemen and Libya, they were no longer welcome there, as was the case in Germany in the 1930s. Many left, some forcibly, necessitating leaving behind possessions and investments.[8]

Of this 850,000, there are no statistics as to the current whereabouts of them and their descendants, because all were absorbed into Jewish society, whether in Israel, or the USA, or elsewhere. *There are no Jewish refugee camps.* Interestingly, this 'forgotten exodus' has been called, by some, the Jewish "Nakba". Israeli columnist, Ben-Dror Yemini had this to say:

"However, there is another Nakba: the Jewish Nakba. During those same years [the 1940s], there was a long line of slaughters, of pogroms, of property confiscation and of deportations against Jews in Islamic countries. This chapter of history has been left in the shadows. The Jewish Nakba was worse than the Palestinian Nakba. The only difference is that the Jews did not turn that Nakba into their founding ethos. To the contrary."[9]

And this brings me to my main point. *Why are there still Palestinian refugee camps? Why weren't the Palestinian Arabs absorbed into one of the many Arab nations that dominate the region*, in particular those countries that host the camps, such as Syria, Lebanon and, in particular, Jordan? One can ask the same question today, regarding the Syrian refugees. Again they are not being re-settled by their brother Muslims, but allowed to be an issue for "Christian" Europe. What is *really* going on here?

There are two players here, in both situations, and neither of them are Jewish … or European. Firstly, there are the *innocents*, those who have been displaced, have become refugees, a fact of history that stretches back through millennia. Population displacements are a consequence of war and conflict, always have been, always will be. As the *Encyclopaedia Britannica* lists in its entry for "refugee":

"Politically motivated refugee movements, frequent in modern times, have occurred intermittently since the development of governments powerful enough to oppress nonconformist

minorities. The Russian Revolution of 1917 and the post-revolutionary civil war (1917–21) caused the exodus of 1.5 million opponents of communism. Between 1915 and 1923 more than 1 million Armenians left Turkish Asia Minor, and several hundred thousand Spanish loyalists fled to France in the wake of the 1936–39 Spanish Civil War. When the People's Republic of China was established in 1949, more than 2 million Chinese fled to Taiwan and to the British crown colony of Hong Kong. The 1950s were marked by the Korean War (1950–53), the Hungarian Revolution (1956), the Cuban revolution (1959), and the Chinese take-over of Tibet (1959), all of which resulted in the flight of more than a million refugees. Between 1945 and 1961, the year that the communist regime erected the Berlin Wall (opened 1989), more than 3.7 million refugees from East Germany found asylum in West Germany. Several major refugee movements have been caused by territorial partition. After the defeat of Germany in World War II, for example, the Potsdam Conference of 1945 authorized the transfer of German minorities from a number of European countries, and 12 million Germans were dumped on the truncated territory of Germany, which was split into east and west regions. The partition of the Indian subcontinent in 1947 resulted in the exchange of 18 million Hindus from Pakistan and Muslims from India – the greatest population transfer in history. Some 8–10 million persons were also temporarily made refugees by the creation of Bangladesh in 1971."[10]

Yet for some reason the United Nations have made a special case of the Palestinians, with the *United Nations Relief and Works Agency for Palestinian Refugees in the Near East* (UNRWA), *the only agency dedicated to helping refugees from a specific region or conflict.*[11] It's curious, isn't it, in the context of the constant stream of refugees spanning the Earth at any given time. Muslim Syria has created, at the time of writing, 13.5 million refugees, over 18 times the number created by the events in Israel in 1948!

So, from the innocent to the *guilty*, those who not only have contributed to creating the situation in the first place, but who are unwilling to accept responsibility for the consequences. This is the leadership of the Arab world, in particular those who were quite happy to allow a nation to fester in camps for over 60 years, in order to sustain a conflict that could have been resolved if humanitarian impulses had outweighed a desire to destroy the Nation of Israel. The greatest victims of all of this are not the Jews, but the innocent Palestinian Arabs, never allowed to thrive and prosper, but kept in forced captivity by their own leaders, in order to fester hatred and ill-will towards Israel, their *perceived enemy*.

And nothing has happened to alleviate the situation. Israel is surrounded by engineered hatred, powered by at least three generations of conditioning. And this hatred has spilled over into world affairs, with Israel presented as aggressor. Strings are being pulled and many others have been sucked into this sad, unnecessary drama. We will next look at the already-mentioned global agency that has had a central role to play in this drama ...

NOTES

1 http://lostislamichistory.com/the-nakba-the-palestinian-catastrophe-of-1948/

2 https://en.wikipedia.org/wiki/Palestinian_refugees#cite_note-d-1

3 https://en.wikipedia.org/wiki/Palestinian_refugees#cite_note-Chiller-Glaus-14

4 https://en.wikipedia.org/wiki/Palestinian_refugees#cite_note-UNRWA-CampProfiles-13

5 https://en.wikipedia.org/wiki/Palestinian_refugee_camps#List_of_camps

6 https://en.wikipedia.org/wiki/Israeli_Jews#cite_note-SelaMain-45

7 https://en.wikipedia.org/wiki/Jewish_exodus_from_Arab_and_Muslim_countries#cite_note-1

8 https://en.wikipedia.org/wiki/Jewish_exodus_from_Arab_and_Muslim_countries#cite_note-4

9 https://en.wikipedia.org/wiki/Jewish_exodus_from_Arab_
   and_Muslim_countries#cite_note-311
10 https://www.britannica.com/topic/refugee
11 https://en.wikipedia.org/wiki/UNRWA

CHAPTER 4

What's with ...
the United Nations?

The time: November 29th 1947. **The place:** United Nations General Assembly. **The occasion:** Voting to decide on the UN Partition Plan to create a Jewish State and an Arab State in the Middle East.

Fifty seven nations voted. Naturally the Muslim countries – Egypt, Iran, Iraq, Lebanon, Pakistan, Saudi Arabia, Syria, Turkey, Yemen and Afghanistan – voted against the plan, not wanting any official declaration of a Jewish nation in their midst. Britain, to its shame considering its century-old relationship with the Jews, abstained; wounded pride at its failure in the area, the "British Mandate" had come to a welcome end. The biggest mystery concerned the attitude of Russia, which actually saw the Jewish Zionists, with their socialist leanings as potential allies in the Middle East. So Russia and its allies joined with Europe and most of the free World and voted for the partition plan. Without this unexpected support, the United Nation partition plan would never have been accepted, as it needed a two thirds majority to be carried through. It was carried through, and the State of Israel was born into the international community.

But this particular midwife was not into post-natal nurturing, in fact it was a most reluctant sponsor of this fledgling Jewish nation and has shown its true colours in the years since. It is earthily summarised by a lowly Spanish interpreter in an unguarded garbled accidental broadcast during a session of the UN General Assembly in November 2013:

"I mean, I think when you have five statements, not five, like a total of ten resolutions on Israel and Palestine, there's gotta be something, c'est un peu trop, non? [It's a bit much, no?] I mean I know... There's other really bad shit happening [around the world], but no one says anything about the other stuff."[1]

Her remarks were an observation that yet again the UN had convened in order to pass a series of resolutions condemning Israel, without a single resolution against not just Palestine but *any other global issue.*

In another comically tragic episode, in 1952 Israel put forward a proposal for a cease-fire in Korea. This was rejected until Norway replaced Israel as sponsor, leading the Israeli representative, Abba Eban to later remark: *"If Algeria introduced a resolution declaring that the earth was flat and that Israel had flattened it, it would pass by a vote of 164 to 13 with 26 abstentions."[2]*

This is no joke, but there's a group within the United Nations that has become one. It is the *United Nations Human Rights Council* (UNHRC). Here is how it describes itself:

"The Human Rights Council is an inter-governmental body within the United Nations system responsible for strengthening the promotion and protection of human rights around the globe and for addressing situations of human rights violations and make recommendations on them. It has the ability to discuss all thematic human rights issues and situations that require its attention throughout the year. It meets at the UN Office at Geneva. The Council is made up of 47 United Nations Member States which are elected by the UN General Assembly."[3]

So far so good. Let's examine these 47 member states that each serve on the Council on a three year term. To get quickly to the point I am just going to concentrate on those from the Asia/Middle East region. China and Saudi Arabia have served four times; Indonesia, Qatar and Pakistan have served three times; UAE, Jordan and Bahrain have served twice; Iraq has served once; *Israel has never served*. Apparently, in this region of the World, one's membership is in direct proportion to the scale of one's human rights offenses. It's like putting a fox in charge of the chicken coop!⁴

Now here's the funny (tragic) point, pointed out on the Wikipedia page:

"As of 2015, Israel has been condemned in 62 resolutions by the Council since its creation in 2006 – the Council has resolved more resolutions condemning Israel than the rest of the world combined. By April 2007, the Council had passed eleven resolutions condemning Israel, the only country which it had specifically condemned. Toward Sudan, a country with human rights abuses as documented by the Council's working groups, it has expressed "deep concern".

The council voted on 30 June 2006 to make a review of alleged human rights abuses by Israel a permanent feature of every council session. The Council's special rapporteur on the Israeli–Palestinian conflict is its only expert mandate with no year of expiry. The resolution, which was sponsored by Organisation of the Islamic Conference, passed by a vote of 29 to 12 with five abstentions. Human Rights Watch urged it to look at international human rights and humanitarian law violations committed by Palestinian armed groups as well. Human Rights Watch called on the Council to avoid the selectivity that discredited its predecessor and urged it to hold special sessions on other urgent situations, such as that in Darfur."⁵

There can be only one of two conclusions, mirroring the one made in the previous chapter. Either Israel is the most evil rogue state in the World or there is a conspiracy of nations 'out to get them!'

The situation is best summarised by a petition currently organised by *UN Watch*, with the following text:

"Contrary to the equality guarantee of the UN Charter, the

UN General Assembly continues to single out democratic Israel by 20 one-sided resolutions each year in the General Assembly – when murderous tyrannies Iran, Syria, and North Korea receive only one each.

Likewise, at the UN's Human Rights Council, Israel is the only country in the world to be targeted under a special agenda item – at every meeting. Former UN chief Ban Ki-moon rightly condemned this act of bigotry.

And this same council keeps a permanent investigator into "Israel's violations." Worse yet, the person they appointed to this post, Michael Lynk, swore that he was impartial, yet UN Watch revealed that he failed to disclose his board memberships on three partisan, pro-Palestinian organizations that lobby against Israel.

It's time to stand up for justice and end the UN's obsession with targeting Israel with an endless amount of absurdly lopsided resolutions – while the real human rights violators instead get elected to high positions, such as Saudi Arabia's absurd election, by a 79% UN majority, to the UN Human Rights Council.

I urge you and other world leaders to demand that the UN puts an end to this discrimination, as its own Charter rules and principles require."[6]

So evidence of some kind of conspiracy seems to be undeniable, unless you are inclined to believe that Israel is 20 times more evil than the abusive regimes in Iran, Syria and North Korea.

My last piece of evidence for an anti-Israel conspiracy within the United Nations emerges from an unexpected source, UNESCO, the *United Nations Educational, Scientific and Cultural Organisation*. It's like being bashed to death by the bugler of the opposing army. The issue is Jerusalem, the ancient capital of the Jewish Nation since it was conquered by King David around 3,000 years ago.

In October 2016 UNESCO passed a decision to not just deny this fact but to declare that Jewish (and Christian) claims to the city are so irrelevant that the very names of historical sites in Jerusalem must only be those associated with the Arab/Muslim tradition. It was making the declaration that *we are henceforth going to deny the Judeo-Christian origins of Jerusalem* and was a subtle attempt to delegitimise Jewish claims on the Land of Israel. This ridiculous notion compels us to ignore truckloads of historical artefacts dug up over recent years that prove the Jewish heritage. This initiative was submitted by Algeria, Egypt, Lebanon, Morocco, Oman, Qatar and Sudan, which was unsurprising. What was surprising was the fact that eight European states, including France, Italy and Spain, abstained and *thus allowed the resolution to be passed!*[7]

For once common-sense seems to have prevailed, with Irina Bokova, the current UNESCO director-general, reaffirming the historical connection between the Jews and their capital:

"The protection of the heritage of Jerusalem is part of a broader vision for peace and the fight against all forms of denial of Jewish history, delegitimization of Israel and anti-Semitism, "[8]

There seems to be an 'about-face' here, which is welcoming, although Ms Bokova actually received death threats because of this stance.[9] But this sorry episode shows how easy it seems that truth can be sacrificed to make a point. Conspiracy eh? What do you think? How we think is governed by the raw information that we consume. And who provides us with this information? We shall look at this next …

NOTES

1 https://www.theguardian.com/commentisfree/2013/nov/28/australia-is-right-to-challenge-the-uns-anti-israel-bias

2 https://www.forbes.com/2010/06/23/israel-hamas-middle-east-opinions-columnists-daniel-freedman.html

3 http://www.ohchr.org/EN/HRBodies/HRC/Pages/AboutCouncil.aspx

4 https://en.wikipedia.org/wiki/United_Nations_Human_Rights_Council#Members

5 https://en.wikipedia.org/wiki/United_Nations_Human_
   Rights_Council#Israel
6 http://secure.unwatch.org/c.bdKKISNqEmG/b.9244463/
   siteapps/advocacy/index.aspx?ievent=153516&action
   =521750
7 https://www.theguardian.com/world/2016/oct/13/israeli-
   anger-unesco-motion-condemning-aggressions-holy-site-
   jerusalem
8 https://worldisraelnews.com/unesco-head-reaffirms-jewish-
   connection-jerusalem/
9 http://www.dailymail.co.uk/wires/afp/article-3845140/
   UNESCO-head-faces-death-threats-Jerusalem-vote-Israel.
   html

CHAPTER 5

What's with ...
the media?

In 1986 a newspaper was born. It was *The Independent*, launched with the slogan, "are you?" Well, I ask ... was it? It may have had independence as its original intention, but, as with every other member of the media, it grew a mind of its own, with its own opinions. It is now independent by name only. It would now regard itself as liberal, in fact in the 2010 election 44% of its readers voted Liberal Democrat.[1]

The fact is that there is no real independence in the media and that we consume (read, watch, listen to) the media that best fits our own views on what is important to us. This is fine as long as we are aware of this fact and don't fall into the trap of believing that the media sources that we have grown up with are not agenda-driven. Until we reach some utopia when all of us are not driven by personal desires and ambitions and view every aspect of the world around us with true neutrality, then we tend to have our opinions fed and watered by like-minded newspaper proprietors, bloggers, talk show hosts, commentators and 'opinion-formers'.

Is there danger in this? Yes, there is, when we see objective truth being compromised in order to sway opinions by whichever means necessary. The ultimate manifestation of this is the recently outed phenomenon of 'Fake news', outright lying and (seemingly) getting away with it. They get away with it in situations when we so wish to believe things in a certain way, *we will do so even if truth gets in the way*!

And nowhere has Fake news been used more insidiously than in the images fed into the western media from Arab Palestinian sources. And this has been going on for decades, with staged photos produced that intend to convey a misleading message, thus twisting the old adage "a picture is worth a thousand words" into a new truism (or false-ism?), "a false picture is worth a thousand words of lies". Here's an example:

There's a picture that has 'done the rounds' of an Israeli soldier pointing a rifle at the head of a Palestinian youth. *Surely here is Israeli aggression against innocent Palestinians!* Another photo appeared, unfortunately too late, of the same two characters, standing together in a friendly selfie. This photo did not do the rounds, suffice to say. The damage had been done, the thousand words of lies had found a fresh seed to germinate.[2]

In April 2002 the media was in a frenzy about the "Jenin Massacre", with news reports from such as the BBC and the *Guardian*, presenting such headlines as *Jenin 'massacre evidence growing'* and clear reporting of a massacre by Israeli forces.[3] A month later, to their credit, the *Guardian* had this to say:

"Despite flimsy evidence British papers jumped the gun to apportion blame when a West Bank refugee camp was attacked, says Sharon Sadeh. As a result, the reputation of the press has been damaged … The battle of Jenin was indisputably fierce and bloody. But while the British papers, almost unanimously, presented it from the outset as a "massacre" or at least as an intentional "war crime" of the worst kind, the US and Israeli papers – Ha'aretz included – were far more reserved and cautious, saying that there was no evidence to back such claims. The left-liberal press in Britain thought differently. The Independent, the Guardian and the Times, in particular, were quick to denounce Israel and made sensational accusations based on thin evidence, fitting a widely held stereotype of a defiant, brutal and don't-give-a-damn Israel."[4]

Apparently one of the drivers for the original emotive reporting by the *Times*, *Telegraph* and *Guardian*, was the obviously flawed testimony of a single individual, Kamal Anis, who claimed to witness Israeli war crimes. The reporters, in a clear dereliction of the independence required in war journalism, heard and believed what they wanted to hear and believe. The *Guardian* article continues:

"Selective use of details or information and occasional reliance on unsubstantiated accounts inflict considerable damage on the reputation of the entire British press, and more importantly, do a disservice to its readers. The US media, especially the press, were wilfully oblivious, prior to the September 11 attacks, to the issues which might have captured more accurately and profoundly the realities regarding the Middle East and the Muslim world, and the appropriate way of approaching and handling them. Are the British media in a similar state of self-denial?"

There is a website called *HonestReporting*, set up to defend Israel from media bias. It is particularly scathing of the British media. They had this to say:

"The UK has been recognized as one of the globe's major centers of anti-Israel activity in the assault on Israel's legitimacy. This is reflected in the amount of material that HonestReporting continues to dedicate to the UK media, which is itself a major contributor to the hostile environment that has encouraged the demonization of Israel and BDS (Boycott, Divestment and Sanctions) campaigns. Media giants such as the BBC have a reach far beyond British shores while outlets such as The Guardian, which displays an outright hostility towards Israel, continue to gain ground with a substantial online readership in the USA. We launched our dedicated HR UK site in 2006 with an eye on the many British media outlets that have consistently shown an anti-Israel bias."[5]

We finish where we started, by turning our attention to *The Independent*, a newspaper that has not just abandoned its 'unique selling point' but has joined the leading ranks of the anti-Israel media. It demonstrated this by commissioning an opinion piece by a certain Ben White, a man known for his unrelenting bias against Israel. Entitled *"Shocked by Donald Trump's 'travel ban'? Israel has had a similar policy for decades"*, it is jam packed with proven 'false news', such as misleading and pejorative descriptions and false claims of torture, with a quote about the Israeli Supreme Court that is the exact opposite of the truth.[6]

The full list is provided in the *HonestReporting* article, *The Independent, Ben White and Alternative Facts* at http://www.honestreporting.co.uk/

Will this anti-Israel bias in the UK ever cease? Following the adage that we just hear what we want to hear, perhaps we have just got the media we deserve, or at least the media that fits in with the mood of the nation? So for things to change, perhaps there needs first to be changes in our society in general?

In the mean-time it is important to get inside the head of those who use the media to tell us why they are so miffed about the State of Israel …

NOTES

1 https://www.ipsos-mori.com/researchpublications/researcharchive/2476/Voting-by-Newspaper-Readership-19922010.aspx
2 http://www.aish.com/jw/mo/Staged-Palestinian-Photos.html
3 http://news.bbc.co.uk/1/hi/scotland/1937048.stm (This news report has not been taken down)
4 https://www.theguardian.com/media/2002/may/06/mondaymediasection5
5 http://honestreporting.com/hr-elevating-action-against-the-uk-media/
6 http://www.independent.co.uk/voices/israel-netanyahu-donald-trump-travel-ban-muslim-ban-a7553141.html

CHAPTER 6

What's with ... the activists?

In our story so far we have seen Israel vilified by the United Nations as an occupying power, with no right to make decisions and laws concerning its own capital and, in terms of the weight of resolutions passed against it, *allegedly the most evil repressive regime on Earth*! Do we *really* believe this? Agendas aside, what is the evidence of those who are promoting such views?

What is under scrutiny are the *actions* of the Jewish State, through the observations of the self-appointed "guardians of human rights", the political and social *activists*. As we saw in the previous chapter, there are many media outlets, particularly those on the left-wing, such as the *Guardian* and *The Independent*, who are quite happy to act as conduits for the views of these activists. So what are these views and why do those on the left-wing have such a problem with Israel?

Well, we have another narrative. It began in the 1960s with the rise of what was called the *New Left*. The "Old Left" were those labour politicians and socialists who welcomed the birth of the Nation of Israel, were in favour of the Balfour Declaration and had firm and friendly ties with the new Nation in its early years. The New Left was a different kettle of fish. They saw the Israelis as colonialists, the latest western colonial power to subjugate the people of the Middle East. *Zionism*, the Jewish aspiration for a safe homeland of their own, now switched from being a socialist dream to a racist ideology, in their view. To the New Left, Israel was nothing more than a white European colony rather than a voted-for sovereign Nation and, as such, needed to be opposed and disbanded and for the "indigenous people" to gain independence. Much of this ideology, unsurprisingly, came from the "other side" of the Iron Curtain, from the Marxism of Soviet Russia and radical rejection of western values was all the rage in the 1960s of The Beatles, flower-power, student demos and eastern mysticism.

This is the backdrop for the promotion of the cause of the Palestinians, even if the conflict was veering towards violence, with the growing phenomenon of plane hijackings. The irony was, and still is, that the support given by the New Left to Palestinian causes, was not centred on left-wing ideologies but rather, with groups such as *Hamas* and *Hezbollah*, motivated by Islamic ideology. The common hatred for Israeli "colonialism" is enough to create the strangest of bedfellows.

What was now needed was to dig up "facts" to promote their views and justify their antipathy. The narrative demanded proof of this "racist State of western colonialists" subjugating the Arab population. Israel must be shown to be an "apartheid state", based on racial segregation between Arabs and Jews. Jimmy Carter, US president in the 1970s, even used this inflammatory term in the title of his book, *Palestine: Peace not Apartheid.*

So is Israel an *apartheid state*? Based on the definition of state-sponsored segregation between different people, as was the case in South Africa, this is simply not true for Israel. Here is a piece from the *Guardian* by someone not particularly known for his sympathies for Israel, yet …

"There are few charges more grave. I should know: during 26 years as a journalist in South Africa I investigated and reported the evil that was apartheid. I saw Nelson Mandela secretly when he was underground, then popularly known as the Black Pimpernel, and I was the first non-family member to visit him in prison. I have now lived in Israel for 17 years, doing what I

can to promote dialogue across lines of division. To an extent that I believe is rare, I straddle both societies. I know Israel today – and I knew apartheid up close. And put simply, there is no comparison between Israel and apartheid. The Arabs of Israel are full citizens. Crucially, they have the vote and Israeli Arab MPs sit in parliament. An Arab judge sits on the country's highest court; an Arab is chief surgeon at a leading hospital; an Arab commands a brigade of the Israeli army; others head university departments. Arab and Jewish babies are born in the same delivery rooms, attended by the same doctors and nurses, and mothers recover in adjoining beds. Jews and Arabs travel on the same trains, taxis and – yes – buses. Universities, theatres, cinemas, beaches and restaurants are open to all..."[1]

Yet many detractors still continue to use the "A" word in relation to Israel, including the United Nations in a report produced unsurprisingly by Arab Nations but not cleared by UN leadership.[2] And it's still not going away, as this recent news report shows, by none other than Ben White, who we met in the previous chapter:

"A new United Nations report accuses Israel of having established "an apartheid regime that oppresses and dominates the Palestinian people as a whole".[3]

How do we answer such views, or is there no smoke without fire? Let us look briefly at the two chief criticisms of Israel by the "activists" of various complexions:

They are building settlements on occupied land! Now there's an agenda-driven sentence. Without delving into ownership issues and the rights of Israelis (whether you see them as conquerors or legal tenants) to conduct these building programmes, why do activists get so hot under the collar? Surely William the Conqueror was free to build wherever he wished in conquered England. Similarly with Napoleon and Alexander the Great. The Jews have been forcibly removed from their ancestral homes many times over the last 2,000 years, most notably from Islamic lands since 1948 and Nazi Europe a few years earlier and Russia and Eastern Europe in the 19th Century. Are all of the Syrian refugees going to be allowed back to their homes, or have many realised that future prosperity may lay elsewhere? Why is there not more of a concerted international effort to relocate Palestinians to lands where they may prosper? These questions may be politically naïve, but surely worth asking?

Also, it is relevant to note that when, in 2005, Israel retreated from Gaza in the interests of peace and forced 8,000 of its own people to leave their "settlements", *Hamas* turned the region into a military outpost and a launching platform for rocket strikes against Southern Israel. Rather than allowing their own people to flourish, they turned the region into a 'pariah state', openly dedicated by their leaders to the destruction of Israel. Surely common sense and the feeling that history tends to repeat itself drives the Israeli leadership into the realisation that allowing the 'West Bank' to be 'Jew free' would result in the same outcome?

They treat the Palestinian Arabs very badly. There is no doubt that things are not that easy for the Arab population of Israel and the "West Bank". But ask most of them whether they would prefer life under the Israelis to life under a Muslim-majority government (as in Gaza) and you will get an answer that the "activists" would prefer to ignore.

In a recent poll of Israeli Arabs (admittedly by an Israeli TV station), 77% of them preferred living under Israeli rather than Palestinian rule. The poll was conducted in Arabic to 405 Israeli Arab citizens by phone.[4] In another poll conducted by the *Palestinian Center for Public Opinion* in Beit Sahour, in the "West Bank", 52% of Palestinians living under Israeli rule in East Jerusalem would prefer to be citizens of Israel with equal rights, with only 42% opting to be citizens of a Palestinian state.[5]

This is action over words, this is the honest opinion of those living in the land compared with the vitriol of agenda-laden activists, who claim to speak for them. Are these the opinions of an oppressed people living in an Apartheid regime?

The focus of our thought should return to these activists. They are clearly people with a passion, but can we dare to suggest that within this passion is a smidgeon of prejudice. Israel is not above reproach and most fair-minded people would suggest that, for more realistic fodder, they should look *not* towards the agenda-ridden United Nations, but instead towards an independent listing such as the report of oppressive regimes by *Freedom House*, that describes itself as *"an independent watchdog organization dedicated to the expansion of freedom and democracy around the world."*

Here is what they said in 2012:

"In this year's Worst of the Worst report, nine countries were identified by Freedom House as being the world's worst human rights abusers in calendar year 2011: **Equatorial Guinea, Eritrea, North Korea, Saudi Arabia, Somalia, Sudan, Syria, Turkmenistan,** *and* **Uzbekistan.** *Two disputed territories,* **Tibet** *and* **Western Sahara,** *were also in this category. All of these countries and territories received Freedom in the World's lowest ratings: 7 for political rights and 7 for civil liberties (based on a 1 to 7 scale, with 1 representing the most free and 7 the least free). Within these entities, political opposition is banned, criticism of the government is met with retribution, and independent organizations are suppressed. Seven other countries fall just short of the bottom of Freedom House's ratings:* **Belarus, Burma, Chad, China, Cuba, Laos,** *and* **Libya.** *The territory of* **South Ossetia** *also is part of this group. All eight, which received ratings of 7 for political rights and 6 for civil liberties, offer very limited scope for independent discussion. They severely suppress opposition political activity, impede independent organizations, and censor or punish criticism of the state."*[6]

While the social and political activists peer at Israel under their microscope, real human rights abusers are getting away with murder ... literally.

We are now going to zero in on a group of people who are extremely vocal about their distaste for the only Democracy in the Middle East.

NOTES

1 https://www.theguardian.com/commentisfree/2015/may/22/
   israel-injustices-not-apartheid-state
2 https://www.washingtonpost.com/news/worldviews/
   wp/2017/03/16/is-israel-an-apartheid-state-this-u-n-report-
   says-yes/?utm_term=.1ec88861015d
3 http://www.aljazeera.com/indepth/features/2017/03/report-
   israel-established-apartheid-regime-170315054053798.html
4 http://www.jpost.com/Arab-Israeli-Conflict/68-percent-
   of-Israeli-Arabs-oppose-recent-wave-of-terrorism-poll-
   finds-382755
5 http://www.washingtoninstitute.org/policy-analysis/view/
   half-of-jerusalems-palestinians-would-prefer-israeli-to-
   palestinian-citizen
6 https://freedomhouse.org/report/special-reports/worst-
   worst-2012-worlds-most-repressive-societies

CHAPTER 7

What's with … academia?

In March 2017, a curious gathering took place in Ireland. It was a conference held at University College Cork and its wordy title was *International Law and the State of Israel: Legitimacy, Exceptionalism and Responsibility*. It was originally scheduled to be held two years earlier at the University of Southampton, but that event was cancelled due to a public outcry, which included a petition and a condemnation from both the local MP and Eric Pickles, the Communities secretary. So in stepped University College …

The conference was organised by a Jewish professor, Oren Ben-Dor. Does that mean that this was going to be a balanced forum, with space given to defenders of the State of Israel? Unfortunately, no. A clue is provided by his views and actions over his academic career. Here is a quote from one of his books:

"The Zionist victim and supremacist mentality – that living force and unity which is nourished by the desire to be hated – stems, before all else, from sublimated hatred of, and supremacy towards, all 'others'."[1]

The organisers highlighted the fact that as many of the contributors were Jewish, this bestowed 'fairness' on the proceedings, yet of the 47 contributors (including the Jewish ones), the majority were anti-Israel activists and there were only two who spoke up for Israel, Professor Alan Johnson and

Professor Geoffrey Alderman, neither of whom were included on the original cast-list at Southampton and only added as a sop to the protestors.[2]

The opening keynote speaker was Richard Falk, a known scourge of Israel, who once posted a grossly offensive anti-Semitic cartoon on his blog, drawing condemnation from all quarters, including David Cameron, the UK Prime Minister.[3]

Here are some of the Jewish participants. Dr Marcelo Svirsky is an activist who wrote *From Auschwitz to Sderot: the decline of our humanity*, a title that makes his position clear. Dr Mazen Masri, who served as a legal advisor to the PLO. Dr Victor Kattan, who is an active supporter of the Palestinian position and the boycotting of Israeli goods. Ms Lea Tsemel, who is described by the BBC as the Israeli who defends suicide bombers.[4]

One of the main closing statements of the conference regarded the issue of apartheid:

"Apartheid is a strong term, but justified. Professor Richard Falk's keynote speech highlighted the meaning of the term, derived from South African historical white rule and discussed his recently-published UN report (with Professor Virginia Tilley), immediately suppressed, which dispassionately considers this question in light of law and policy in Israel before concluding that the term is a justified one."[5]

The 'suppression' of this report was actually its rejection and withdrawal by UN chief, Antonio Guterres, but when a 'dispassionate' report has been sponsored by a world body, ECSWA, made up in its entirety of 18 Arab states, you don't expect it to be exactly impartial (or dispassionate)!

So, what do we have here? We have a group of academics, with an impressive string of qualifications, drawn from all over the World, eager to make a unified statement about an entity for which they had a mutual hatred. The idea was to provide legitimacy for their cause, which was to de-legitimise the State of Israel. *After all, surely such a bunch of clever people couldn't be wrong, could they?* I would suggest that the fact that this meeting was held in a University ranked 283rd in the World[6] does not provide too much kudos and implies that the other 282 (apart from Southampton) had wisely told them to *sling their hook!*

We should stop for a moment and consider the fact that we have just read about a conference held for the sole reason of suggesting that a sovereign state, because of its perceived actions, has no right to exist among the 193-strong family of nations. What about other states? Are we saying that Israel is such a pariah state among such paragons of virtue and human rights as North Korea, Iran and Saudi Arabia that it is the only one to warrant an international meeting of minds to question its very reason for existence? If you google the words 'delegitimising nations' you will find 14,200 results and, after leafing through the first dozen or so pages, *the only nation mentioned is Israel*, with links to both sides of the debate. There is either something so unprecedentedly evil about this particular nation or ... it has a lot of enemies bent on its destruction! You decide.

But, moving on, we have been dealing here with the 'usual suspects', a group of like-minded people on an academic jolly in pleasant surroundings having a *good ol' rant*. They can be excused, in a way, as they were simply expressing the views they have developed over a lifetime of experiences. But what of the rest of 'academia'? What's their problem with Israel? Because there surely is a problem. Let's rewind 15 years ...

On April 6th 2002, a couple of academics from the Open University decided that a response was needed to show displeasure at Israel's "violent oppression against the Palestinian people". It took the form of an open letter in the *Guardian*, printed here:

"Despite widespread international condemnation for its policy of violent repression against the Palestinian people in the Occupied Territories, the Israeli government appears impervious to moral appeals from world leaders. The major potential source of effective criticism, the United States, seems reluctant to act. However there are ways of exerting pressure from within Europe.

Odd though it may appear, many national and European cultural and research institutions, including especially those funded from the EU and the European Science Foundation, regard Israel as a European state for the purposes of awarding grants and contracts. (No other Middle Eastern state is so regarded). Would it not therefore be timely if at both national and European level a moratorium was called upon any further such support unless and until Israel abide by UN resolutions and open serious peace negotiations with the Palestinians, along the lines proposed in many peace plans including most recently that sponsored by the Saudis and the Arab League."[7]

Thus began the beginning of the academic boycott of Israel in this country. Within three months 700 academics had signed up and words translated into actions when Professor Mona Baker of UMIST in Manchester decided to sack two Israeli academics from working on her journal for the sole reason of their country of origin.[8] Three years later the *Association of University Teachers* voted to boycott two Israeli Universities on very shaky premises. This decision was later reversed after a huge backlash, partly prompted by the fact that the initial vote was made purposely at Passover time, to ensure a low Jewish attendance and that the decision wasn't thoroughly debated "through lack of time allocated".[9]

This may have been a setback for the movement but it didn't stop the *National Association of Teachers in Further and Higher Education* from passing a motion in May 2006 to boycott any Israeli academics who were not public in condemning their own government.[10] Thankfully good sense prevailed and the resulting kerfuffle involved the general secretary of the association receiving over 15,000 messages from opponents, including a condemnation from the British government.[11] But it didn't end there when the *University and College Union* (formed by the merging of the two associations) voted for an academic boycott of Israel in May 2007.[12]

In December 2013 the boycott of Israeli academic institutions was finally joined by the *American Studies Association* (ASA), a respected organisation devoted to the study of American culture and history. One must ask what Israel has to do with American history and it is telling that it is the first nation it has ever boycotted in the 52 years of existence of the ASA![13] When asked why Israel was so singled out, the ASA president, Professor Curtis Marez responded, *"We have to start somewhere"*.[14]

And so this sorry tale of the "academonising" of Israel continues and shows no sign of slowing down. A letter to the *Guardian* from Paul Miller a few years ago put the absurdity of the situation most succinctly (leaving aside the questionable premise):

"Israel's occupation of Palestinian land is intolerable but the academic boycott by the page of signatories is disturbing in its selectivity. China occupies Tibet, India occupies Kashmir, Turkey occupies Northern Cyprus and Russia occupies Crimea and eastern Ukraine. Moreover, many countries, such as Saudi Arabia and Egypt, have the most extreme abuses of human rights. In boycotting only the Jewish state those signatories evoke frightening memories of past boycotts of Jewish institutions."[15]

What is it with these academics? Have their huge brains short-circuited their sense of fairness and common sense? Why are they so selective in their ire? We should not don our rose-tinted specs and suggest that Israeli academia itself is whiter-than-white or that, for whatever reasons, there aren't injustices against Palestinians. That is not the point of this book. The question I ask and that will be repeated constantly is *why a disproportionate focus on Israel?* It's a theme that, as you are seeing, operates far beyond the academic world.

In the next chapter we are going to see thoughts and ideas translating into actions ...

NOTES

1 Holy Land Studies, Apr 2012, vo. 11, No. 1 : pp. 33-62
Occupied Minds: Philosophical Reflections on Zionism,

Anti-Zionism and the Jewish Prison Oren Ben-Dor

2   The inconvenient fact that a large number of speakers and some audience participants were themselves Jewish, from Israel and from the Diaspora …Point 9 on CLOSING STATEMENT https://israelpalestinelaw.com/closing-statement/

3   https://en.wikipedia.org/wiki/Richard_A._Falk#Accusations_of_antisemitism

4   http://news.bbc.co.uk/1/hi/world/middle_east/3087051.stm

5   https://israelpalestinelaw.com/closing-statement/

6   UCC is ranked 283th in the current edition of the QS World University Rankings   https://www.topuniversities.com/universities/university-college-cork

7   https://www.theguardian.com/world/2002/apr/06/israel.guardianletters

8   https://www.theguardian.com/uk/2002/jul/08/highereducation.israel

9   https://web.archive.org/web/20060130124019/http://www.kcl.ac.uk/kis/unions/aut/council.htm

10 https://web.archive.org/web/20060914152824/http://commentisfree.guardian.co.uk/brian_klug/2006/05/drawing_a_line_in_the_sand.html]

11 https://www.theguardian.com/education/2006/jun/20/internationaleducationnews.highereducation

12 https://www.theguardian.com/uk/2007/jun/09/highereducation.israel1

13 https://www.insidehighered.com/news/2013/12/17/american-studies-association-backs-boycott-israeli-universities

14 http://www.wiesenthal.com/atf/cf/%7B54d385e6-f1b9-4e9f-8e94-890c3e6dd277%7D/TOP-TEN-2013.PDF

15 https://www.theguardian.com/world/2015/oct/28/academic-boycott-of-israel-is-misguided

CHAPTER 8

What's with ...
the boycotters?

Think about kids in a playground. What's the best way to show disdain for a classmate? You bully him and make his life hell. Now, what's the best way to make him feel lonely and unwanted? You ignore him, *even if* he's offering the best snacks and/or homework copying service. We've seen the former in the World's disdain for Israel. Now we're going to meet the latter. Welcome to the world of the boycotters.

According to Wikipedia there have only been six country-specific boycotts in recent history. If we ignore Nazi Germany, Cuba, apartheid South Africa and the mutual boycotting of Russia and Ukraine, there is only one country left, out of the Global family of 196 nations, and that is *Israel*. Quelle surprise![1]

Who is doing the boycotting and why? Yes, it's the usual suspects. First off, the *academics*, who we have just met. In a rare show of solidarity with their teachers, the *students* aren't far behind, joining our growing rabble of unusual bedfellows, all united in their hatred of Israel.

The *National Union of Students* (NUS), in their online student guide ("filling you in on life and fun at uni!"), passed a vote *to boycott companies with Israeli sympathies, as well as products made in the country.* It "justifies" this action with the usual blanket statements, regarding settlements, Israel's military capacity and alleged human rights abuses. It also conceded that

Nestle and Coca-Cola products would also need to be removed from campus, making sensible people wonder what connection this may have with human rights issues etc.[2]

Then there are those involved in the entertainments industry, notably Roger Waters (Pink Floyd), Brian Eno (Roxy Music) and the violinist, Nigel Kennedy. Waters demands an artistic boycott of Israel until a list of conditions are met, including the right of return of all Palestinian refugees.[3] In February 2015, 700 entertainers said they would boycott Israel until its "colonial oppression of Palestinians" ended, drawing parallels to apartheid-era South Africa.[4]

The World Council of Churches joined the party in 2001, followed by the Presbyterian Church in the USA, the United Church of Christ and the United Methodist Church. In 2009 the *Kairos Palestine document* was drawn up by Palestinian Christians, bringing God into the political arena and "assuring" the World that the "occupation" was a "sin against God".[5]

All of these actions eventually found a point of focus in 2005 with the Palestinian-led *Boycott, Divestment and Sanctions movement* (BDS), that modelled itself on the anti-apartheid movement that opposed the racist regime in South Africa. They now self-declare as a "vibrant global movement made up of unions, academic associations, churches and grassroots movements across the world" and, to be consistent with the on-going narrative of previous chapters, stress the two prejudicial triggers of *apartheid* and *colonisation*.[6]

BDS found a surprising critic in the form of Norman Finkelstein, scourge of the Zionists. Here's what he said in an interview with a French pro-Palestinian activist:

"'I loathe the disingenuousness – they don't want Israel [to exist],' he said. 'It's a cult.' He had spent his time in a self-deceptive Maoist cult, he said; he wouldn't do it again. He accused BDS activists of 'inflating the numbers' of Palestinian refugees and 'want[ing] to create terror in the hearts of every Israeli' rather than resolve the conflict. 'I'm not going to tolerate what I think is

silliness, childishness, and a lot of left-wing posturing,' he said."[7]

There is something very unsavoury about the whole business. It gives an impression that BDS and such initiatives serve to focus the energies of those who enjoy protesting for its own sake and Israel has been chosen as a soft target. But that's just my observation.

It seems that in some cases the making of a political point is even more important than the livelihood of those that, allegedly, the boycott is meant to help. Take the case of *SodaStream*. This Israeli company operated in the "West Bank" and was a persistent target for BDS. The company employed many Palestinian Arabs, who benefited greatly from the higher than average wages and benefits. Now it has had to re-locate, seen as a triumph by BDS, but not by the hundreds of Palestinian employees, who are now faced with an extra four hours of travelling to work daily, including crossing an Israeli checkpoint![8]

I cannot finish this topic without mentioning the following very poignant and cutting observation by comedian Sam Levinson regarding Israeli boycotts. It may make us chuckle but the truth within its message exposes the hypocrisy of BDS and its bedfellows (this bed is getting very large!):

"It's a free world; you don't have to like Jews, but if you don't, I suggest that you boycott certain Jewish products, like the Wasserman test for syphilis; digitalis, discovered by a Dr. Nuslin; insulin, discovered by Dr. Minofsky; chloral hydrate for convulsions, discovered by Dr. Lifreich; the Schick test for diptheria; vitamins, discovered by Dr. Funk; streptomycin, discovered by Dr. Z. Woronan, the polio pill by Dr. A. Sabin and the polio vaccine by Dr. Jonas Salk. Go on, boycott! Humanitarian consistency requires that my people offer all these gifts to all people of the world. Fanatic consistency requires that all bigots accept syphilis, diabetes, convulsions, malnutrition, infantile paralysis and turberculosis as a matter of principle.You want to be mad? Be mad! But I'm telling you, you ain't going to feel so good!"[9]

In the same vein, here are some observations on the same issue by Aish.com on their website, with reference to any conference convened to further the boycott cause:

"Bring plenty of pens, pencils and notebooks – the old fashioned kind. No lap top computers and no cell phones allowed. After all, the Intel microchip processor, network firewalls, Microsoft NT and XP, keyboards for smart phones, flash drives, the ability to print straight from a computer, and much of cell phone technology were all developed by the Zionist entity. But look at the bright side: you won't have to remind people to silence their cell phones during presentations of such exciting academic papers as "Class and Gender Fault Lines within the Neo-Colonial White Male Establishment in the Occupy Movement … Bring lots of books for your free time. Anyone trying to smuggle an Amazon Kindle to the conference will have it confiscated. Its Operating System is yet another Zionist conspiracy. And don't even think about logging onto your Facebook account from the hotel's business center; much of the Facebook software ecosystem was developed in Tel Aviv, the Silicon Valley of the Middle East. To help you whittle down your reading choices, omit Jewish authors. Voila! Your reading options have just gone on an extreme diet."[10]

Many of you would have noticed, perhaps indignantly, that, in the sorry picture being painted so far in this book, there are some names that perhaps shouldn't be there. This curious phenomenon will be explored in the next chapter.

NOTES

1   https://en.wikipedia.org/wiki/Category:Boycotts_of_ countries
2   http://www.thestudentguide.com/survival_guide/article/nus_ vote_to_boycott_israeli_goods
3   https://en.wikipedia.org/wiki/Boycotts_of_Israel#cite_note-92
4   https://www.indy100.com/article/seven-hundred-artists-

have-just-announced-a-cultural-boycott-of-israel--eySdBeqw2g

5 https://en.wikipedia.org/wiki/Kairos_Palestine

6 https://bdsmovement.net/what-is-bds

7 https://newrepublic.com/article/122257/unpopular-man-norman-finkelstein-comes-out-against-bds-movement

8 https://www.theguardian.com/world/2015/sep/03/sodastream-leaves-west-bank-as-ceo-says-boycott-antisemitic-and-pointless

9 http://articles.chicagotribune.com/1995-09-07/features/9509070083_1_dear-abby-discovered-boycott

10 http://www.aish.com/j/fs/Go-Ahead-Make-My-Boycott.html

CHAPTER 9

What's with …
some Jews?

Here's a partial cast-list of protagonists in our story so far: Norman Finkelstein, Noam Chomsky, Oren Ben-Dor, Dr Marcelo Svirsky, Dr Mazen Masri, Dr Victor Kattan, Lea Tsemel. The two things they all have in common are their negativity towards Israel … and their *Jewishness*. How come? Let's backtrack a bit, first.

It is probably worth considering first the key founding statement for the State of Israel. On July 5th 1950, the Law of Return was passed. Its purpose was to re-iterate the key purpose of the State of Israel itself.

"The State of Israel was established for the very purpose of repatriating the Jewish people from the Diaspora, to enable the "Ingathering of the Exiles", to give every Jew anywhere in the world the option to return to the land of his fathers. Two thousand years of wandering were officially over. The Law of Return (and related Law of Citizenship) states that every Jew in the world has the inherent right to settle in Israel as an automatic citizen; it emphasizes the purpose of Israel as a homeland for all Jews."[1]

History has shown that no Jew is truly safe in the World at large, that no society has ever fully protected their interests. It is an insurance policy for those Jews in the *Diaspora*, in case it all goes 'belly up' and they start to sniff the wind of intolerance, as so many missed in "civilized" Germany in the 1920s and

1930s. Whatever one's views of the moral foundation, political machinations and 'human rights' record of the State of Israel, the emotional attachment, sneaking comfort and sense of loyalty it surely invokes in the heart of every Jew should surely outweigh every other consideration. There are two things to take into account here:

1. The hatred shown to Jewish people by a wide spectrum of humanity is historically unprecedented. The presence of one small place on Earth where this hatred can have no effect is surely warranted.
2. Any perceived evils committed by the State of Israel, as hopefully this small book has shown, is miniscule compared to those committed by the majority of nations in the World, in particular its nearest neighbours.

Yet despite these two points, there are many Jews, some even living in Israel, and most of them highly educated, who continue to fight against the best interests of the Jewish homeland, who seem to have succumbed to the same propaganda of those who at least have anti-Semitism (even if it isn't acknowledged) as a reason for their hatred! It feels a little bit like that cartoon of the tree-feller with a chainsaw busy slicing through the branch that he is sitting on!

Is it possible to be a self-hating Jew? There's a Wikipedia page for it[2] so it seems to be an acknowledged phenomenon. It is even suggested that it is "a neurotic reaction to the impact of antisemitism by Jews accepting, expressing, and even exaggerating the basic assumptions of the anti-Semite."[3] There's surely a whiff of the "Stockholm syndrome" effect, where victims under siege befriend their besiegers?

In the UK there is a group called Jews for Justice for Palestinians that describes itself as "advocating for human and civil rights, and economic and political freedom, for the Palestinian people".[4] It has done a lot to rally together British Jews from the arts and academia, many of them famous names, in petitions against the actions of Israel. It is tempting to judge these people, but all we can hope for is that each is acting according to their conscience and that their sense of justice is ultimately going to be informed by the truth and not propaganda.

But there are other groups that take this even further. They are Jews, many actually living in the land, who would prefer that *Israel didn't exist in the first place!* These are groups within orthodox Judaism that have a distinct disdain for the modern secular world and particularly for the State of Israel. One of these groups, *Neturei Karta,* even proudly displays an Israeli flag being burned on the home page of their website[5] and make this statement on their website:

"We seek to live in the land of Palestine as anti-Zionist Jews. To reside as loyal and peaceful Palestinian citizens, in peace and harmony with our Muslim Brethren."[6]

What is the issue with such groups? It is a theological one. They believe that the formation of the State of Israel is a human endeavour, rather than a divinely orchestrated supernatural event. For this reason they declare the State of Israel invalid and Zionism an evil philosophy. Their fierce opposition to Israel is not so much about how it operates, as a sovereign nation in the secular world, *but by the very fact of its existence.* Incredibly, they share the same aim as *Hamas,* no less than the destruction of the State of Israel! This view is not shared by the majority of ultra-Orthodox groups within Judaism, who number around 20,000 in Israel and a few thousand more in the USA and Europe.

NOTES

1 http://www.palestinefacts.org/pf_1948to1967_lawofreturn.php

2 https://en.wikipedia.org/wiki/Self-hating_Jew

3 https://en.wikipedia.org/wiki/Self-hating_Jew#cite_note-Lewis-13

4 https://en.wikipedia.org/wiki/Jews_for_Justice_for_
   Palestinians
5 http://www.nkusa.org/
6 http://www.myjewishlearning.com/article/ultra-orthodox-
   anti-zionist/

CHAPTER 10

Now it gets personal

So far we have experienced the phenomenon of anti-Israelism or anti-Zionism. Yet what is really at the heart of all of this? I am reminded of burglars who declare that their thieving is not really a crime against a person, as the insurance companies are the ones that take the hit! There is a denial concerning the real victims by offering a smokescreen to obscure the true intentions. Simon Schama describes this well:

"The charge that anti-Zionism is morphing into anti-Semitism is met with the retort that the former is being disingenuously conflated with the latter. But when George Galloway (in August 2014 during the last Gaza war) declared Bradford 'an Israel-free zone'; when French Jews are unable to wear a yarmulke in public lest that invite assault, when Holocaust Memorial day posters are defaced, it is evident that what we are dealing with is, in Professor Alan Johnson's accurate coinage, 'anti-semitic anti-Zionism'."[1]

So let's not beat around the bush here. Anti-Israelism and anti-Zionism are just politically correct versions of *anti-Semitism*, pure and simple. All we see since the birth of the Nation of Israel in 1948, is a convenient channelling of the ancient hatred that is more acceptable at soirees and around dinner tables.

It is time to get personal, to switch from corporate expressions to individual focus and where better to start than inside the mind of a Jihadist.

NOTES

1 http://antisemitism.org.il/article/103641/left's-problem-jews-
   has-long-and-miserable-history

CHAPTER 11

What's with … Jihadists?

A *jihadist* is "one who struggles", which is quite intriguing as the Hebrew understanding of the word *Israel* is of "struggling with God". There is a real sense of a struggle between Jew and Muslim Arab, all the more intriguing as they share a common ancestor, Abraham from the Bible (and the Quran), and trace their lineage back to his sons, the half-brothers Isaac and Ishmael.[1]

Since the time of Muhammed, the relationship between Jew and Muslim has been a rocky one, apart from the short period within the 8th Century known as the *Golden Age of Jewish culture in Spain*, when the Muslim rulers were far more benign towards the Jewish population than their Christian counterparts elsewhere in Europe. Sadly this is not so in modern times and most of the current problems can be traced back to 1928, to the founding of the *Muslim Brotherhood* by Hasan al-Banna, an Islamic "back-to-basics" movement. There was a sinister element to this, as the movement were ardent supporters of Nazi Germany, freely distributing Arabic translations of *Mein Kampf* at an Arab Muslim conference in Egypt in 1938. Their intentions are expressed here by Professor David Patterson of the University of Texas:

"By 1945 they had become a hybrid of Nazism and Islam to form Islamic Jihadism, making the extermination of the Jews not just a political or territorial aim but a defining element of their

worldview: one cannot be part of the Brotherhood or any other Islamic Jihadist group, just as one cannot be a Nazi, without espousing the extermination of the Jews."[2]

Why such hatred towards the Jewish people, after all the Nation of Israel hadn't yet come into the equation? Professor Patterson continues:

"If the Jihadist Bible is the Quran, and not Mein Kampf, then the Jihadist evil transcends the Nazi evil, inasmuch as the Quran is Scripture, a revelation from God, and not just the pronouncements of the Führer. Establishing a scriptural foundation for their actions, the Jihadists can justify any action. Eclipsing God, the Nazis eclipse the absolute prohibition against murder imposed from beyond, so that the inner will and imagination from within posed the only limits to their actions. By contrast, appropriating God, the Jihadists appropriate the authority to impose what they have determined to be the will of Allah, which is not a matter of human will but an absolute obligation."

So the question remains is whether the Muslim holy book, the *Quran*, compels them to hate Jews, or whether the hatred comes first? In truth it appears to be a mixture of both. There certainly are passages in the book that seem prejudicial to Jews, to say the least:

"Amongst them we (Allah) have placed enmity and hatred till the Day of Judgment. Every time they kindle the fire of war, Allah doth extinguish it; but they (ever) strive to do mischief on earth. And Allah loveth not those who do mischief."[3]

"When in their insolence they transgressed (all) prohibitions, We said to them: 'Be ye apes, despised and rejected'."[4]

Although there are also verses in the Quran that are better disposed towards the Jews, the principle of "progressive revelation" demands that these are cancelled out by the later, nastier ones. But it is in the later commentaries, the *hadiths*, that we see some of the main damage, particularly this one about the *final slaughter of the Jews.*

"(Muhammad said:) The last hour would not come unless the Muslims will fight against the Jews and the Muslims would kill them until the Jews would hide themselves behind a stone or a tree and a stone or a tree would say: Muslim, or the servant of Allah, there is a Jew behind me; come and kill him; but the tree Gharqad would not say, for it is the tree of the Jews."[5]

According to the Answering Islam website, we must be mindful as to how this is played out in the current enmity between the Arab Muslim world and Israel.

"This apocalyptic belief of a future battle against Israel and the murder of all Jews is a deeply held belief among many Muslims. And we must remember that these anti-Semitic traditions and verses from the Quran are over a thousand years old. These sacred Islamic traditions of a final slaughter of all Jews cannot be attributed to the present day conflict with the State of Israel. As much as many today try to blame Muslim enmity toward Jews solely on Zionism and its alleged "Nazi-like" abuse of the victimized and oppressed Palestinians, it simply cannot be done in an honest and informed manner. The enmity of Islam toward the Jews has existed since Islam's inception. It is not a new phenomenon. And today Islam and the Muslim world is undeniably the single most anti-Semitic force on the earth. Palestinians in particular, use the anti-Semitic apocalyptic template as a basis for much of their actions toward Israel and the Jews today."[6]

So it is an ancient hatred, revived in modern times and using the Israel/Palestine conflict as an excuse. Certainly Muslims throughout history have not had a persistent and active hatred of Jews at all times, as the self-proclaimed *Golden Age* mentioned earlier demonstrated. Arguably Jews have had far more antagonism from the Christian world over the last 2,000 years. Yet the hatred seems to lurk behind the scenes, just below the horizon, waiting to attach itself to a cause. Israel, since 1948, has provided such a cause, for those looking for a justification for the anger they feel.

It must be stressed that it is very much the minority of Muslims who are affected by this, just as not all academics, Christians, activists etc. are automatically to be tarred by the brush of anti-Semitism.

But the "God-factor" is a compelling one for some, as we shall see in the next chapter ...

NOTES

1 Chronicles 1:28
2 http://isgap.org/flashpoint/nazis-jihadists-and-jew-hatred/
3 Surah 5:64
4 Surah 7:166
5 *Sahih Muslim Book 041, Number 6985*
6 http://www.answering-islam.org/Authors/JR/Future/ch13_islams_ancient_hatred.htm

CHAPTER 12

What's with ...
the Christians?

This may come as a shock to some of you. There are some Christians who *actually like Jewish people* and are not the slightest bit inclined to hate them. This is one of the saddest and ironic statements one could have to make because any correct understanding of the Bible, both Old and New Testaments, identifies the Jewish people as 'God's eternal and chosen people'.

"For You have established for Yourself Your people Israel as Your own people forever, and You, O LORD, have become their God."[1]

"I say then, God has not rejected His people, has He? May it never be! ... God has not rejected His people whom He foreknew ..."[2]

Yet not all Christians see it this way. Here is a quote from a 4th Century "church father", John Chrysostom nicknamed the "golden-mouthed":

"The synagogue is not only a whorehouse and a theatre; it is also a den of thieves and a haunt of wild animals ... not the cave of a wild animal merely, but of an unclean wild animal ... The Jews have no conception of things at all, but living for the lower nature, all agog for the here and now, no better disposed than pigs or goats, they live by the rule of debauchery and inordinate gluttony. Only one thing they understand: to gorge themselves and get drunk."[3]

Golden-mouthed? You wouldn't want to see him on a bad day! Unfortunately history has seen the "Church" on many a bad day, when words translated into actions, when rhetoric gave rise to persecution, expulsions and massacres.

Where does all this hatred come from? The Bible? The words of Jesus? It's as if history is playing a massive joke on us ... and it ain't funny! We are presented with this 1st Century Jew who preached love and forgiveness and with a Bible that reminds us of God's favour towards the Jews. Yet ... Jesus' followers chose to ignore both and, arguably, this situation *still remains today* in these "enlightened" times. Here's a piece of evidence.

On February 16th 2002 the journalist, Melanie Phillips wrote an article in *The Spectator* entitled *Christians who hate the Jews.* She was reporting on a meeting of Jews and prominent Christians brought together to discuss the churches' increasing hostility towards Israel. She wrote:

"The real reason for the growing antipathy [to Israel], according to the Christians at that meeting, was the ancient hatred of Jews rooted deep in Christian theology and now on widespread display once again ... The Jews at the meeting were incredulous and aghast. Surely the Christians were exaggerating. Surely the Churches' dislike of Israel was rooted instead in the settlements, the occupied territories and Prime Minister Ariel Sharon. But the Christians were adamant. The hostility to Israel within the Church is rooted in a dislike of the Jews." (my emphasis).

"The Christians at that meeting affirming this view were the editor of the main Church of England newspaper, the Archbishop of Wales (later the Archbishop of Canterbury), the Middle East representative of the Archbishop of Canterbury and the head of a Christian institute and relief organisation, who remarked 'What disturbs me at the moment is the very deeply rooted anti-Semitism latent in Britain and the West. I simply hadn't realised how deep within the English psyche is this fear of the power and influence of the Jews."[4]

So this 'longest hatred' is still present in a Church that no longer blames Jews for killing Jesus, or desecrating communion wafers, or poisoning wells, or kidnapping Christian children. Yet there is still an element within this multinational organisation that doesn't like Jewish people. Here are some examples, as listed by Wikipedia:

"The *World Council of Churches* (WCC) has been described as taking anti-Zionist positions in connection with its criticisms of Israeli policy. In February 2016, the *General Assembly of the Presbyterian Church of USA* was urged by one of its own committees to support the *Boycott, Divestment and Sanctions* (BDS) movement against Israel. John Stott, a well respected UK Christian teacher said, *"Political Zionism and Christian Zionism are anathema to Christian faith... The true Israel today is neither Jews nor Israelis, but believers in the Messiah, even if they are Gentiles ..."* In April 2013 the *Church of Scotland* rejected the idea of a special right of Jewish people to the Holy Land through analysis of scripture and Jewish theological claims. In July 2010, the *UK Methodist Conference* called for a boycott of Israeli goods ..."[5]

Let's cut to the chase and try and get inside the head of one of those Christians who still inclines towards a negative attitude of the Jews and Israel, even if they may deny it, or perhaps are even unaware of it because they prefer not to even think about it.

The driving force seems to be the theology they have constructed to counteract the two Bible quotes quoted at the head of this chapter, in order to *de-mystify* the Jewish people, to strip away any perceived divine 'chosen-ness'. At the heart of this is the thought, *hey aren't we God's chosen people now, God can't have two chosen people, that makes no sense to me!* And if they can convince themselves of this, then they are free to exercise their prejudices, secure that they are not angering their God.

So are they right? Yes, if they believe that their God can change his mind after making a promise. And why would they believe this?

The story begins in the 2nd Century with a man declared a heretic by his Christian peers. His name was Marcion and he believed that things of religion can be split into two parts, the old rejected part and the new favoured part. In the former he would place the Old Testament, the *God* of the Old Testament and the *people* of the Old Testament, the Jews. In the latter, the place of favour would belong to the New Testament, the *God* of the New Testament (Jesus) and the *people* of the New Testament, the Christians. With a stroke of his twisted pen he had created a mandate for centuries of "Christian" anti-Semitism. He was excommunicated but his discredited and faulty ideas live on today.

Marcion's ideas are followed, mostly unacknowledged, by those Christians who emphasise the New Testament so much that they diminish the relevance of the Old Testament in the life and theology of the Church today. Their constant refrain is that "the Old must be re-interpreted in the light of the New", leading to the key thought that *that which is attached to the Old must be replaced by that which is attached to the New*. In other words, the "new" people of God, the *Christians*, replace the "old" people of God, *the Jews*. It may have seemed a good idea, with centuries of traditions and rhetoric to back it up, but a more critical view of history would have revealed the *consequences* of such teachings, being the persecutions, expulsions and massacres. The two go together and neither surely could be condoned by a God of love and forgiveness. These people are on shaky ground if they believe that their God is happy with such a situation. But then they seek to justify their attitude by reference to the Bible.

The crux is this: The Bible is admittedly a difficult book to understand and interpret. Christians are told to ask God to help them in this task – and most do. But it is also tempting to fall back on traditions, on accepted teachings, with the attitude that *who am I to go against teachings that have been around for centuries?* There is no excuse, each must be led by their own conscience here. They need to re-evaluate everything in the light of history ... and the consequences of these teachings.

The good news though is that there are a growing number of Christians worldwide (though not so many in the UK!) who, along with the great preachers of yesteryear such as Charles Spurgeon, John Wesley, A. W. Tozer, Martin Lloyd-Jones and J.C. Ryle, if we were in a position to ask them ... believe that this chapter should never have needed to be written!

Next we have a chapter that most definitely had to be written ...!

NOTES

1 2 Samuel 7:24

2 Romans 11:1-2

3 Chrysostom, John, *Eight Orations against the Jews*, 1, 3, 4

4 Phillips, Melanie *Christians who hate the Jews*. The full article can be seen on http://melaniephillips.com/christians-who-hate-the-jews

5 https://en.wikipedia.org/wiki/Anti-Zionism

CHAPTER 13

What's with ... neo-Nazis?

There's one thing following an ideology that resulted in millions of Jews (and others) perishing in concentration camps, but to continue to promote a modern-day version that denies the existence of these camps is to be in a very dark place indeed.

In 1945 British troops liberated one of these camps and here is a transcript of an account by one of the soldiers, Dick Williams:

"But we went further on into the camp, and seen these corpses lying everywhere. You didn't know whether they were living or dead. Most of them were dead. Some were trying to walk, some were stumbling, some on hands and knees, but in the lagers, the barbed wire around the huts, you could see that the doors were open. The stench coming out of them was fearsome. They were lying in the doorways – tried to get down the stairs and fallen and just died on the spot. And it was just everywhere. Going into, more deeper, into the camp the stench got worse and the numbers of dead – they were just impossible to know how many there were...Inside the camp itself, it was just unbelievable. You just couldn't believe the numbers involved... This was one of the things which struck me when I first went in, that the whole camp was so quiet and yet there were so many people there. You couldn't hear anything, there was just no sound at all and yet there was some movement – those people who could walk or move – but just so quiet. You just couldn't understand that all

those people could be there and yet everything was so quiet…
It was just this oppressive haze over the camp, the smell, the
starkness of the barbed wire fences, the dullness of the bare
earth, the scattered bodies and these very dull, too, striped grey
uniforms – those who had it – it was just so dull. The sun, yes the
sun was shining, but they were just didn't seem to make any life
at all in that camp. Everything seemed to be dead. The slowness
of the movement of the people who could walk. Everything
was just ghost-like and it was just unbelievable that there were
literally people living still there. There's so much death apparent
that the living, certainly, were in the minority."[1]

This is a fruit of the Nazi ideology, the practical personification
of pure hatred. The focus in this discussion ultimately lies at the
feet of Adolph Hitler and the reasons for this hatred. There has
been a move in modern times to look for personal motivations for
his rabid animosity towards the Jews. Some have suggested that
a Jew may have abused his grandmother, or that a Jewish doctor
may have misdiagnosed his mother's cancer that killed her.[2] But a
reading of *Mein Kampf* makes it clear that his hatred derived from
Germany's loss in the First World War, for which he blamed the
Jews, both for their prominence in international finance and in
the Communist movement. This hatred had no rational basis and
he justified it by convincing himself, then his followers (followed
by most of Germany) that the Jews, along with Gypsies and Slavs
and others, were a biologically inferior race to the Aryans, the
white northern Europeans. Just as with the African slave trade in
earlier times, once a whole race has been dehumanised, it is easy
to persecute and maltreat them and even plot their destruction.

It was all meant to change when the horrors of the Holocaust
were revealed to the World through newsreels, reporting from
the front-line, victim testimonies and the Nuremberg war crime
trials. But the virus of anti-Semitism can be a tough critter to
dislodge if the host body is comfortable with it. So the shattered
ideology of Nazism went dormant, kept below the radar for a
while, then re-emerged as neo-Nazism.

Here is the story in the UK. After laying low for nine years, this ideology entered the public arena as the *League of Empire Loyalists* in 1954, a pressure group opposed to the dissolution of the British Empire and led by a leading fascist, Arthur Chesterton. Its core belief was that Russian Bolshevism and American-style Capitalism were actually working together as a Jewish conspiracy against the British Empire! This group led to the formation of the *British National Party* (BNP) in 1960. After some internal splits this group morphed into the *National Front* (NF) in 1967. This became the biggest far-right political party in the UK in the 1970s and gained a degree of acceptance in some working-class areas, even polling 44% in a local election in Deptford. This group soon declined in the 1980s and the *British National Party* re-emerged in 1982, still with us today.

When Nick Griffin took over the party he tried to water down the anti-Semitism promoted by the party. He said: *"we can get away with criticising Zionists, but any criticism of Jews is likely to be legal and political suicide."*[3] A pragmatic statement, rather than a change of heart! In their literature, reference to Jews was obscured through the use of the term "Zionists" and there are various references to an unnamed "group of conspirators" who have worked against the nationalistic elements of British society and are even responsible for the *Islamification* of the country![4]

So the old hatreds are still there, despite the testimony of history that shows the outcome of such hatreds. This is all swept under the carpet through the twisted viewpoint known as *Holocaust denial*. In order to try and normalise their hatreds, the best solution these people can come up with to address the situation in Nazi Europe in the 1940s, is to actually deny that it ever happened, despite the overwhelming evidence, not the least from survivors of the Holocaust. Holocaust denial is so insidious that it has been declared illegal in several countries, including Austria, Germany, Hungary and Romania that were perpetrators of the Holocaust. There have been numerous convictions of individuals who have fallen foul of these laws and have received hefty fines or imprisonment, including Jean-Marie Le Pen, father of the high-profile French politician, Marine Le Pen.

For neo-Nazis, the justification for their anti-Semitism has been wrapped up in their concocted conspiracy theories regarding the Jewish people. These are going to be explained in more detail in the next chapter.

NOTES

1 http://www.iwm.org.uk/sites/default/files/public-document/Liberation_Bergen_Belsen_Transcript.pdf

2 http://www.haaretz.com/jewish/news/why-did-adolf-hitler-hate-the-jews-1.2618

3 https://en.wikipedia.org/wiki/British_National_Party#cite_note-FOOTNOTETrilling201285-169

4 https://en.wikipedia.org/wiki/British_National_Party#cite_note-FOOTNOTERichardson201152.E2.80.9353-201

CHAPTER 14

What's with ...
Conspiracy buffs?

In an era when "fake news" has actually become a genre itself, the number of "conspiracies" regarding the Jews have reached a peak. At least it is not always as bad as it was in earlier times, in "Christian" Europe, when "fake news" had *terrible consequences*. The first was probably the most damaging and far-reaching, that *the Jews killed Christ*. This insidious lie still pops up in some ignorant backwaters and places the responsibility for the death of Jesus firmly at the feet of every Jew who has ever lived, despite the fact that the crucifixion was a Roman punishment actually carried out by Roman soldiers[1] and that Jesus not only went willingly to his death[2] but publicly forgave everyone responsible[3]. This inconvenient truth hasn't stopped this accusation being responsible for the persecution and deaths of thousands of Jews for the last 2,000 years. But it didn't end there. Jews were blamed for poisoning wells and causing the Black Death, for kidnapping and killing Christian children and desecrating communion wafers. All had ... *consequences*.

We love conspiracies, whether involving moon landings, the deaths of presidents, movie stars or princesses, or fevered speculations about items of complete trivia, dreamed up by media moguls to increase circulation figures. Then there are the outlandish theories of who exactly is pulling the strings in the World today. Many candidates have been put forward, from the disguised lizards of David Icke, to the secret societies of the Freemasons, the Illuminati, the Jesuits, the Bilderbergs, the Knights Templar, the Rosicrucians, the Club of Rome and ... yes, of course, the Jews.

And we're not talking of just one alleged Jewish conspiracy, there's a whole swathe of them. Whispers are heard of the *Protocols of the Elders of Zion*. Zionism is seen as a front for World domination, with the Israeli secret service (*Mossad*) pulling the strings. Then there are the Illuminati, the Freemasons, the United Nations, the New World Order, the Communists, the International Monetary Fund (IMF), the World Bank and the World's press. Apparently all have been sucked into the Jewish web! Jews have been put forward as the primary cause of most of the major problems that have weakened European society in the past 200 years such as: World War I, World War II, communism, socialism, liberalism, capitalism, mass immigration, forced integration, racial preference laws, and media bias. Such busy bees, we've been!

The *Protocols of the Elders of Zion* is probably the most well known weapon in the armoury of anti-Jewish conspiracy nuts. It is also a *complete forgery*, but why should the truth get in the way of a good yarn? It is claimed to be the minutes of a meeting of Jewish leaders at the first Zionist congress in Basel, Switzerland in 1897 (or, as some say, a graveyard in Prague), when the Jews were hatching an audacious plot to take over the World!

What it actually was is not that easy to follow. It seems to be based on a pamphlet written at the turn of the 20th Century by a Russian forger as a means to discredit reforms in that country and bolster the influence of the Czar. This forger took material from a satire on Napoleon III by Maurice Joly and from a novel by Hermann Goedesche, a 19th Century German anti-Semite. The final form of the Protocols first appeared in Russia in around 1905, becoming a best seller by 1920 and promoted in the USA by none other than Henry Ford, who when he wasn't building cars was ranting and raving about Jews. It was first exposed as a forgery by Philip Graves of the *Times* in 1921, not before one Adolph Hitler had a chance to read it and believe it. Possibly after noticing that car sales were plummeting in parts of New York, Henry Ford was forced to make a public retraction, admitting that the book that he wrote in 1920, *The International Jew*, was based on the Protocols.[4]

Of course anti-Semites of all persuasions are not going to let the fact that it is pure fiction get in their way as it is freely distributed these days by Muslim hate groups and neo-Nazis. A popular Egyptian TV series, *A Knight without a horse*, is even based partly on it – there's a scene where three old Jews are sitting in a room filled with religious artefacts and are heavily perspiring and conspiring as they plot and plan.[5]

Naturally the Nazis made good use of the Protocols as a justification for their paranoid hatred of the Jews. Since then, their main use has been as justification for Arab nationalism, in the Muslim hatred against the State of Israel. The Protocols were translated into Arabic from the French edition probably in the late 1920s and by the 1950s the forgery could be found all over the Arab world, from Cairo to Beirut. They were even authenticated by Egyptian president Nasser, and his brother published a new edition in 1968, under the title, *Brutukulat Hukama Sahyun wa-Ta`alim at-Talmud* (Protocols of the Learned Men of Zion and Teachings of the Talmud).

Hamas actually refers to the Protocols in article 32 of its charter:

"The Zionist plan is limitless. After Palestine, the Zionists aspire to expand from the Nile to the Euphrates. When they will have digested the region they overtook, they will aspire to further expansion, and so on. Their plan is embodied in the "Protocols of the Elders of Zion", and their present conduct is the best proof of what we are saying."[6]

Most of the other so-called Jewish conspiracies are simply variations on the theme or *strategies* to achieve World domination over the last few hundred years. Let's summarise a few of them:

- in 1775 Jews financed the American Revolution.
- in 1933 Jews conspired against the Germans and caused World War II.
- in 1990 Jews conspired against the Iraqis and caused the Gulf War.
- in 1999 Jews conspired to incite the bombing of Serbs in Serbia
- in 2001 Jews were the real instigators of 9-11.
- Jews have instigated, supported and financed World War I, the Cold War, the Korean War, the Vietnam War as part of a perpetual Jewish war against the rest of the World.

There are some who believe that Jews control the USA and Europe, through an organization known as ZOG (Zionist Occupation Government). This term first appeared in 1976 through the pen of a neo-Nazi called Eric Thomson. Since then it has reappeared with increasing frequency, in the rants of various groups, such as the *Aryan Nations* in the USA and hateful websites such as *Jew Watch*.

Just think, if all the above were true, it speaks as much about Gentile stupidity as it does of Jewish cunning, blindly allowing themselves to be led through every major calamity in history by just 0.19% of the World's population. It was this kind of thinking that made the "Final Solution" against the Jews acceptable to the German mind in the 1930s. It was forced into their minds through every possible channel of propaganda until one was unable and unwilling to disbelieve it. It made it possible for ordinary Germans to turn a blind eye, first to the expulsions and exclusions, then to the shop burnings and Jew-baiting and finally to journeys in cattle wagons to far off places in Poland, never to be seen again.

Finally, the most repulsive, sinister and intellectually corrupt claim of all; the one that affirms that the Holocaust never happened, despite thousands of Jewish (and Gentile) eye witnesses, Nazi documents, newsreels and other photographic evidence. They suggest that the Holocaust was a Jewish conspiracy, a lie simply to engender sympathy from the World for the Jewish plight and yearning for a homeland of their own. One such Holocaust-denier, David Irving, sued an American academic, Deborah Lipstadt, in 2002 for claiming that he is a 'Hitler partisan' who twists history to cast the German dictator in a better light. He lost his case and his house and was declared bankrupt.

The Jews have indeed been a busy people! Conspiring to take over the World through their cunning and deviousness, while the rest of the World is powerless to resist them in wide-eyed innocence.

Talking of conspiracies, what is less well known are the ones that are *against* Jewish people. The plots and subterfuge initiated against the Nation of Israel, by friend and foe alike, could furnish plots for a dozen Frederick Forsyth novels. In fact the insistence of a Jewish conspiracy to control the World is a conspiracy itself, if the truth be told. One day the truth *will* be told and then there will be many heads hung in shame. Until that day we'll just have to put up with the fact that ZOG controls the White House, the Pope is a secret Jew and the Hollywood film industry is just a front for the Israeli Secret Service!!!

NOTES
1 Matthew 27:27-31
2 Matthew 20:17-19
3 Luke 23:34
4 http://www.jewishvirtuallibrary.org/jsource/anti-semitism/ ford.html
5 https://www.gazetawarszawska.com/judaizm-islam/1249-a-knight-without-a-horse
6 https://en.wikipedia.org/wiki/Contemporary_imprints_of_ The_Protocols_of_the_Elders_of_Zion#cite_note-HAMAS-charter-23

CHAPTER 15

What's with … ?

Yes, there are more. No, it hasn't ended yet, we haven't yet worked our way through the full cast list, though we have covered the main players. To lead us into this and to remind us of our central message, here's a telling snippet from *The Tablet* magazine in September 2013:

"No other group of people on the planet is accused so much and of such fantastic wrongs. For a few decades after the Holocaust, it seemed that anti-Semitism might wane or even die out. That hope has now been defeated. Could anything we do or say stem the tide, or will Jew-hatred persist as long as there are Jews to hate?"[1]

In the previous chapter we looked at the various conspiracy theories (or rather 'fancies') centred on Jews. The majority of them are in fact deflectors from the shortcomings of the instigators, using the Jews as an excuse for their own failings. The word used in this context is 'scapegoat'.

The concept of the *scapegoat* is a Jewish one. It was one of the two goats received by the Jewish high priest in ancient Jerusalem on the Day of Atonement, as described in Leviticus 16. The priest laid his hands upon the scapegoat as he confessed the people's sins, before sending it out into the wilderness. Today, a person who has been blamed for something which is the fault of another is referred to as a scapegoat. The Jews have always been a convenient scapegoat for others, allowing them to ignore their own shortcomings or giving them a channel to vent their frustrations and misfortunes. By blaming Jews for every low point in human history, from the Black Death, to communism to the Second World War, it may make one feel superior and justified, but it's doing nothing more than feeding a lie.

For instance, the reason why Jews were blamed for the Black Death in medieval Europe was because so few of them actually succumbed to the plague. The real reason for this was the laws of cleanliness practiced by the Jewish people. They were just cleaner than the 'Christians' and so were less likely to catch certain diseases. Capitalists blamed the Jews for Communism while Communists blamed them for Capitalism! And so it goes on.

Jews may have had stricter standards of hygiene but, what really got the hackles up were the fact that, statistically, they were also cleverer than the average 'Christian'. Here are some amazing statistics:

There are just over 14.3 million Jews worldwide (2015 figures), indicating that about *0.19% of the World is Jewish* – about 1 person out of every 520.[2] Yet, according to Wikipedia:

"*Nobel Prizes have been awarded to 881 individuals, of whom 197–22.4% – were Jewish or people of Jewish descent although Jews and people of Jewish descent comprise less than 0.2% of the world's population ... Jews or people of Jewish descent have been recipients of all six awards, including 41% of economics, 28% of medicine, 26% of physics, 19% of chemistry, 13% of literature and 9% of all peace awards.*"[3]

So we move into awkward areas here. These are uncomfortable facts for those with certain theories about the superiority of races and we can only suggest that jealousy has given rise to resentment. To counter this one should also ask how many Jews have excelled in other fields of endeavour, such as sport!

This leads to one issue that sits very uncomfortably with some "religious" people. It's the issue of *chosenness*. The attitude is conveyed in the way the term is used. *One of the chosen people, eh?* If there's the hint of a snarl, then there's an issue. It's as if Jewish people *choose* to be chosen! It's a no-win situation, there are some "Christians"[4] who will clobber you equally for being *chosen* and for being *rejected*! It says more about *their insecurities* than any perceived "superiorities" of the Jewish people.

This is also a problem with atheists, who will also have an issue with the "one doing the choosing" and would take out their resentment on the objects of this "choosing by a non-existent deity".

One particular conspiracy theory does have a measure of truth in it, though one needs to dig deeper to see how the situation first arose. This is the issue of money and finances, one of the biggest areas of resentment against Jews, where we even find a verb "to jew" defined as *to bargain shrewdly or unfairly. To haggle so as to reduce a price.*[5]

Isn't that amazing? Here are a people, chosen by God as a "kingdom of priests" when most other people were either sacrificing their babies to idols or praying to stone figures for rain or fertility. And yet these very same Jewish people are acknowledged through a verb associated with the seamier underbelly of shady dealings. And as for the measure of truth mentioned earlier, the reason why the Jewish people are good with money, as typified by the great banking dynasties of the Rothschilds, Montagues, Hambros, Samuels etc., is that this was *virtually the only profession the Christian world allowed them to practice*. If you do something well for a very long time, you are going to get good at it! Out of this dominance of the financial systems came the conspiracy theories, which are still with us today.

The first Jews to arrive in England came in 1066 with William the Conqueror and they were the financiers who helped the Normans administer their conquered land. To the natives of the land they were 'outsiders', they looked different, they spoke differently and they lived in their own communities, forced into this situation through "Christian" fear and hatred. To many they are still *outsiders*.

Question: *Why do you Jews tend to live separately in your own communities?*

Answer: *Because you forced us to in the first place!*

The first *ghetto* was in Venice, an enclosed part of the city where Jews could be segregated from the rest of the population. In medieval times many European cities had such a place, which was convenient for Himmler, the Nazi leader who, in June 1943, who ordered them dissolved and transformed into concentration camps.

With this knowledge of the advanced apartheid conditions that the Jews were forced to endure for so much of their history, it brings a sense of proportion to such modern initiatives as *Israel Apartheid Week*. This is an initiative of University students worldwide, starting in Toronto in 2005. It has even been held in Jerusalem! The organisers said the week has: *"played an important role in raising awareness and disseminating information about Zionism, the Palestinian liberation struggle and its similarities with the indigenous sovereignty struggle in North America and the South African anti-Apartheid movement."*[6]

The wording of this statement, with such trigger words as "liberation" and "struggle" (twice), is pure Marxist rhetoric and leads to confusion as to the political agenda being followed here. At the time of writing right-minded people in the academic world are starting to weary of this and there's an astute comment in a recent article in the *Daily Telegraph* by Richard Black:

"This year is especially fraught because it marks the centenary of the Balfour Declaration, a document issued in 1917 which first proclaimed Britain's commitment to the establishment of a "national home for the Jewish people". The fact that IAW (Israel Apartheid Week) has decided to fixate on this event speaks

volumes. It shows their issue is not with Israeli occupation or this or that policy. Its abiding objective is to undo a century of Jewish self-determination in the Middle East. ... IAW almost universally promotes a simplistic approach to discussions of the conflict. It characterises Israel as an 'apartheid' state and a 'settler-colonial' regime. It is nothing of the sort. As Professor Derek Penslar has elaborated, Israel has resembled post-colonial patterns of state building, respectively in terms of its Zionist emphasis on national liberation, and in terms of the trajectory of its twentieth-century political, social and economic development. South African journalist and veteran anti-Apartheid activist Benjamin Pogrund has also argued that the apartheid analogy is baseless in international law. He has described the charge as "at best, ignorant and naïve and, at worst, cynical and manipulative". There is simply no systematic state system of white supremacy in the democratic State of Israel. Arab citizens enjoy total legal and political equality."[7]

So ... what's with? This story just goes on and on. It never finishes, but this book *has* ... almost.

NOTES

1 http://www.tabletmag.com/jewish-arts-and-culture/books/143487/academic-anti-semitism

2 https://en.wikipedia.org/wiki/Jewish_population_by_country

3 https://en.wikipedia.org/wiki/List_of_Jewish_Nobel_laureates

4 You will notice that I make a distinction between Christians and "Christians". It is sad to relate that much of the history of the Church has been dominated by "Christians" rather than by true believers in the faith instigated by Jesus the Jewish messiah

5 http://www.thefreedictionary.com/Jew

6 https://en.wikipedia.org/wiki/Israeli_Apartheid_Week

7 http://www.telegraph.co.uk/education/2017/03/02/british-universities-have-duty-jewish-students-monitor-israel/

CHAPTER 16

Consequences

And it goes on ... and on ... and on. Is there no end to this multi-headed hydra of hatred against the Jews? Our onion has been well and truly peeled! To be honest, this book has only skimmed the surface of the seas of animosity, to give a full picture would fill a bookshelf or three. The objective has simply been to alert people to a massive injustice without laying it on too thickly.

We have reached an uncomfortable truth, that the World, for whatever reason, just doesn't like Jews. They may veil their hatred by directing their ire towards Israel or Zionism, but it's all the same, just anti-Semitism dressed differently. The key words here are "for whatever reason" and it is these words that are going to lead us deeper into the heart of this problem.

For whatever reason? In the story of Moses and the Exodus, the Egyptian Pharaoh thought he had a reason, *they may grow too large and turn against us.*

For whatever reason? The Church fathers thought they had a reason, *after all the Jews killed Christ, didn't they?*

For whatever reason? In the early days of the Church, Roman emperor Constantine thought he had a reason, *they are encouraging Christianity to remain too Jewish.*

For whatever reason? The medieval Church thought it had a reason, *they steal communion wafers in order to stick pins in them and trample on them, so torturing Christ!*

For whatever reason? The Protestant leader, Martin Luther, thought he had a reason after many years of trying to convince the Jews, *they refuse to convert to Christianity!*

For whatever reason? French rationalist philosopher Voltaire thought he had a reason, *they gave us Christianity!*

For whatever reason? The Nazis and neo-Nazis think they have a reason, *they are an inferior race!*

For whatever reason? The Palestinians think they have a reason, *they have stolen our land!*

For whatever reason? The United Nations, the activists, boycotters, academics and others think they have a reason, *their country is probably the most evil nation in the World!*

There's an awful lot of "for whatever reasons" and I haven't even started on those who blame the Jews for capitalism, communism, 9-11, the two World Wars, polluting the Aryan race, Hollywood (we'll concede that one!) on a list that grows longer year by year.

It's that word "whatever". It tells us that the World will *always* find a reason to hate Jews, it's an unescapable fact and it's unlikely to change soon. And, as history has shown us … there are always *consequences*.

Thoughts usually lead to actions and, although this has rarely been good news, there are people in this World who are not burdened by prejudice, who read the truth … and act on it. Can you be one of these people? The best antidote to lies and prejudice is education in the truth. Hopefully this book has made a difference.

One final thought. There has never been a satisfactory

explanation for anti-Semitism from historians, philosophers, psychologists, sociologists, economists and social commentators, for the simple reason that it seems to be driven by *blind irrational hatred*. Can this really be orchestrated, the greatest conspiracy of all? Is this possible? Where does anti-Semitism come from? Only God Knows!